Horrid Henry's
Annual 2013

Horrid Henry's
Annual 2013

Francesca Simon

Illustrated by Tony Ross

Orion
Children's Books

First published in Great Britain in 2012
by Orion Children's Books
a division of the Orion Publishing Group Ltd
Orion House
5 Upper Saint Martin's Lane
London WC2H 9EA
An Hachette UK Company

1 3 5 7 9 8 6 4 2

This compilation, *Horrid Henry's Annual 2013* © Orion Children's Books 2012
Design by Envy Design Ltd
Text © Francesca Simon 2012
Illustrations © Tony Ross 2012

Compiled by Sally Byford from the *Horrid Henry* books
by Francesca Simon & illustrated by Tony Ross

The Orion Publishing Group's policy is to use papers that are natural, renewable and recyclable
products and made from wood grown in sustainable forests. The logging and manufacturing processes
are expected to conform to the environmental regulations of the country of origin.

A catalogue record for this book is available from the British Library.

Printed and bound in Germany.

ISBN 978 1 4440 0347 5

www.orionbooks.co.uk
www.horridhenry.co.uk

Contents

MWAHAHAHAHAHAHAHAH!

Yo, Fans and Purple Hand Gang members!

It is I, Henry, the world's greatest zombie vampire werewolf hunter in the known universe. Who else but I could see through Miss Battle-Axe's disguise to reveal her true character: a zombie vampire! And Miss Lovely too, definitely a zombie vampire in teacher's clothing. What other monsters are lurking at my school, I wonder? Hmmmm....

Meanwhile, what a year I've had! When I wasn't bravely fighting zombie vampires lurching around Our Town Museum, I got Peter to do ALL my chores and give me ALL his money. Plus I discovered I am a genius story teller – check out *King Hairy the Horrible and Queen Gertrude the Gruesome* if you dare – and quite an amazing chef as well.

So get out your fangs, set your dials to scary, and let's go 2013!

Henry

How Many Vampire Bats?
How many vampire bats can you find hidden in the Annual? Here's the first one.

11

Horrid Henry's Zombie Vampire Resolutions

⭐ **1** Expose Miss Battle-Axe for the zombie vampire she is.

⭐ **2** Tell Peter there's a monster in his wardrobe and a zombie under his bed.

⭐ **3** Make the scariest horror movie ever, called "*The Undead Demon Monster Who Would Not Die.*"

4 Turn Margaret into a zombie ... wait, she already is one – tee hee.

5 Round up all the zombie vampires in the neighbourhood and herd them towards the school. Ha! That should give me a few extra days holiday ...

Brainy Brian's Scary New Year Quiz

1. **When Henry sneaks downstairs in the dark and lands on something lumpy on the comfy black chair, what does he do?**
   (a) He quietly turns on the light to see what it is.
   (b) He screams, 'AAARRRRGGGH!'
   (c) He attacks the lumpy thing with a cushion.

2. **What is a Fangmangler?**
   (a) The slimiest, scariest, most horrible and frightening monster in the whole world.
   (b) The latest gadget for sale in Toy Heaven.
   (c) Something that Henry has made up to scare everyone.

3. **How does Henry try to make Peter look scarier on Hallowe'en?**
   (a) He gives him a scary haircut.
   (b) He cuts off his little bunny tail.
   (c) He makes him wear an evil mask.

4. **Which of Peter's toys is Henry desperate to get his hands on?**
   (a) Bunnykins.
   (b) Snoozy Whoozie, a bunny that giggles you to sleep.
   (c) The Curse of the Mummy Kit.

5. **When Henry has a sleepover at New Nick's, what's the scariest thing that happens to Henry in the night?**
   (a) Nick's little sister, Lisping Lily, tries to kiss him.
   (b) Five wet smelly dogs pounce on him.
   (c) The wind howls through the bedroom window.

14

6. When Henry stays at Great-Aunt Ruby's, he hears a ghostly noise from the wardrobe in the night. What does he do?

(a) He runs crying to Great-Aunt Ruby's room.

(b) He grabs his Goo-Shooter, gets out of bed and flings open the wardrobe door.

(c) He hides under the duvet.

7. What does Henry do to try and get out of having an injection?

(a) He runs away.

(b) He pretends to be ill.

(c) He kicks Nurse Needle.

8. At Perfect Peter's pirate party, Henry invents a pirate to scare Peter? What's he called?

(a) Sammy the Shrunken Head Slug.

(b) The Purple Hand Pirate.

(c) Blood Boil Bob, the cannibal pirate.

Don't be scared. Turn to page 74 to find out the answers.

6 – 8
A sizzling score. Your knowledge is spine-tingling!

3 – 5
You know some fiendish facts, but not enough to be totally terrifying.

1 – 2
AAAAAGH! Your score is so low – it's scary!

Horrid Henry's House of Horrors

DEADLY DUNGEON

Horrid Henry and the Zombie Vampire

"Hello boys and girls, what an adventure we're going to have tonight," said the museum's guide, Earnest Ella, as she handed out pencils and worksheets.

Henry groaned. Boring! He hated worksheets.

"Did you know that our museum has a famous collection of balls of wool through the ages?" droned Earnest Ella. "And an old railway car? Oh yes, it's going to be an exciting sleepover night. We're even going on a torch-lit walk through the corridors."

Horrid Henry yawned and sneaked a peek at his comic book, which he'd hidden beneath his museum worksheet. Watch out, Demon Fans!! To celebrate the release of this season's big blockbuster monster horror film, THE ZOMBIE VAMPIRES, study this check-list.

Make sure there are no zombie-vampires lurking in your neighbourhood!!!!

Horrid Henry gasped as he read *How To Recognise a Vampire* and *How to Recognise a Zombie.* Big scary teeth? Big googly eyes? Looks like the walking dead? Wow, that described Miss Battle-Axe perfectly. All they had to add was big fat carrot nose and . . .

A dark shadow loomed over him.

"I'll take that," snapped Miss Battle-Axe, yanking the comic out of his hand. "*And* the rest."

Huh? He'd been so careful. How had she spotted that comic under his worksheet? And how did she know about the secret stash in his bag? Horrid Henry looked round the hall. Aha! There was Peter, pretending not to look at him. How dare that wormy worm toad tell on him? Just for that . . .

"Come along everyone, line up to collect your torches for our spooky walk," said Earnest Ella. "You wouldn't want to get left behind in the dark, would you?"

There was no time to lose. Horrid Henry slipped over to Peter's class and joined him in line with Tidy Ted and Goody Goody Gordon.

"Hello Peter," said Henry sweetly.

Peter looked at him nervously. Did Henry suspect *he'd* told on him? Henry didn't *look* angry.

"Shame my comic got confiscated," said Henry, "'cause it had a list of how to tell whether anyone you know is a zombie vampire."

"A zombie vampire?" said Tidy Ted.

"Yup," said Henry.

"They're imaginary," said Goody-Goody Gordon.

"That's what they'd *like* you to believe," said Henry. "But I've discovered some."

"Where?" said Ted.

Horrid Henry looked around dramatically, then dropped his voice to a whisper.

"Two teachers at our school," hissed Henry.

"Two *teachers?*" said Peter.

"What?" said Ted.

"You heard me. Zombie vampires. Miss Battle-Axe *and* Miss Lovely."

"Miss *Lovely?*" gasped Peter.

"You're just making that up," said Gordon.

"It was all in *Screamin' Demon*," said Henry. "That's why Miss Battle-Axe snatched my comic. To stop me finding out the truth."

Does Horrid Henry discover the truth about zombie vampires at Our Town Museum? Find out in **'Horrid Henry and the Zombie Vampire'** from **Horrid Henry and the Zombie Vampire**.

Creepy Criss-cross

Can you fit these words into the criss-cross puzzle?

4 letters
OGRE

5 letters
WITCH
GHOST
TROLL

6 letters
ZOMBIE

7 letters
VAMPIRE
MONSTER

8 letters
WEREWOLF

9 letters
HOBGOBLIN

CLUE:
FILL IN THE LONGEST WORD FIRST.

Body Search

Find these body parts in the wordsearch below.

EAR   LIVER
NAIL   MUSCLE
VEIN   ARTERY
NOSE   TONGUE
TEETH   KIDNEY
HEART   EYEBALL

K	N	E	P	N	T	D	Y
R	I	Z	L	E	A	R	X
E	E	D	E	C	E	I	N
V	V	T	N	T	S	O	L
I	H	Z	R	E	S	U	P
L	L	A	B	E	Y	E	M
W	U	T	O	N	G	U	E
D	T	R	A	E	H	D	X

21

How to Hold a Zombie Party

INVITATIONS

- Make invitations out of black card or paper.

- Don't invite any scaredy-cats.

- Write in white chalk or crayon when and where your party will be held.

- Tell your friends to come dressed up as zombies.

- Decorate your invitations by drawing on eyeballs – or sticking on plastic googly eyes.

PARTY FOOD

Finger Sandwiches
Edible Eyeballs
Blood Red Jelly
Blackcurrant Juice

ZOMBIE MAKEOVERS

When your guests arrive, give them all a scary makeover with face paints.

ZOMBIE GAMES

Make a Zombie Giggle

Choose someone to be the Zombie It – Zit for short. All the other players are zombies. They must lie quietly on the floor without moving. Zit has to try to make the zombies giggle – but he's not allowed to touch them! The last zombie left is the winner.

Pin the Eyeball on the Zombie

Draw or print out a large picture of a zombie, and a separate picture of an eyeball. Blindfold your friends in turn, spin them around and see who can pin the eyeball in the right place.

Hunt the Eyeball

Fill a large bowl with cooked spaghetti, and hide ping pong balls in it. Time how long it takes each of your friends to find all the eyeballs.

Zombie Parade

Get all your party guests together for a Zombie Parade. Silently stagger around the house and garden, staring scarily ahead in a zombie-like fashion. See if you can frighten your parents or your little brothers and sisters.

23

Moody Margaret's Fake Blood

Fake blood is fantastic for April Fool's Day! Try Moody Margaret's realistically revolting recipe.

You will need

Golden syrup
Red food colouring
Cocoa powder
Water
Cornflour
A bowl or jar

Instructions

1. Mix a couple of spoonfuls of golden syrup with red food colouring until it's the colour of blood.

2. Add a pinch of cocoa powder to darken the mixture, and make it look more like real blood.

3. If your blood is too thick, add a bit of water. If it's too thin, add a pinch of corn flour and mix it in slowly and carefully.

4. Then it's time to scare your family and friends … Dribble this fake blood from your mouth – it's OK to eat!

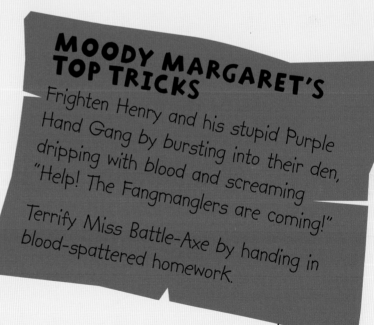

MOODY MARGARET'S TOP TRICKS

Frighten Henry and his stupid Purple Hand Gang by bursting into their den, dripping with blood and screaming "Help! The Fangmanglers are coming!"

Terrify Miss Battle-Axe by handing in blood-spattered homework.

24

How Scared Are You?

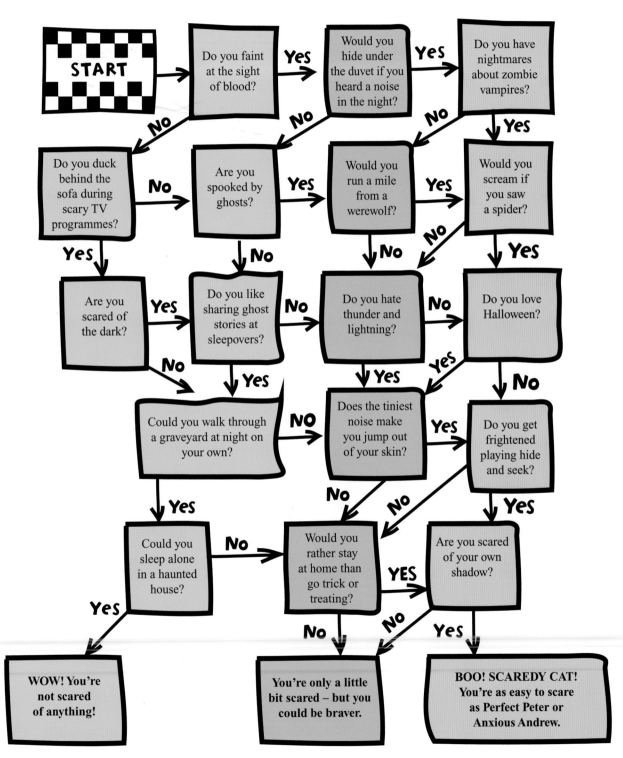

START

Do you faint at the sight of blood? — **Yes** → Would you hide under the duvet if you heard a noise in the night? — **Yes** → Do you have nightmares about zombie vampires?

Do you faint at the sight of blood? — **No** → Do you duck behind the sofa during scary TV programmes?

Would you hide under the duvet if you heard a noise in the night? — **No** → Are you spooked by ghosts?

Do you have nightmares about zombie vampires? — **No** → Would you run a mile from a werewolf?

Do you have nightmares about zombie vampires? — **Yes** → Would you scream if you saw a spider?

Do you duck behind the sofa during scary TV programmes? — **No** → Are you spooked by ghosts?

Do you duck behind the sofa during scary TV programmes? — **Yes** → Are you scared of the dark?

Are you spooked by ghosts? — **Yes** → Would you run a mile from a werewolf?

Are you spooked by ghosts? — **No** → Do you like sharing ghost stories at sleepovers?

Would you run a mile from a werewolf? — **Yes** → Would you scream if you saw a spider?

Would you run a mile from a werewolf? — **No** → Do you hate thunder and lightning?

Would you scream if you saw a spider? — **No** → Do you hate thunder and lightning?

Would you scream if you saw a spider? — **Yes** → Do you love Halloween?

Are you scared of the dark? — **Yes** → Do you like sharing ghost stories at sleepovers?

Are you scared of the dark? — **No** → Could you walk through a graveyard at night on your own?

Do you like sharing ghost stories at sleepovers? — **No** → Do you hate thunder and lightning?

Do you like sharing ghost stories at sleepovers? — **Yes** → Does the tiniest noise make you jump out of your skin?

Do you hate thunder and lightning? — **No** → Do you love Halloween?

Do you hate thunder and lightning? — **Yes** → Does the tiniest noise make you jump out of your skin?

Do you love Halloween? — **Yes** → Does the tiniest noise make you jump out of your skin?

Do you love Halloween? — **No** → Do you get frightened playing hide and seek?

Could you walk through a graveyard at night on your own? — **NO** → Does the tiniest noise make you jump out of your skin?

Could you walk through a graveyard at night on your own? — **Yes** → Could you sleep alone in a haunted house?

Does the tiniest noise make you jump out of your skin? — **Yes** → Do you get frightened playing hide and seek?

Does the tiniest noise make you jump out of your skin? — **No** → Would you rather stay at home than go trick or treating?

Do you get frightened playing hide and seek? — **No** → Would you rather stay at home than go trick or treating?

Do you get frightened playing hide and seek? — **Yes** → Are you scared of your own shadow?

Could you sleep alone in a haunted house? — **No** → Would you rather stay at home than go trick or treating?

Could you sleep alone in a haunted house? — **Yes** → **WOW! You're not scared of anything!**

Would you rather stay at home than go trick or treating? — **YES** → Are you scared of your own shadow?

Would you rather stay at home than go trick or treating? — **No** → **You're only a little bit scared – but you could be braver.**

Are you scared of your own shadow? — **No** → **You're only a little bit scared – but you could be braver.**

Are you scared of your own shadow? — **Yes** → **BOO! SCAREDY CAT! You're as easy to scare as Perfect Peter or Anxious Andrew.**

25

Horrid Henry's Top Ten Scary Moments

10 The day I was forced to go on a walk in the countryside by my mean, horrible parents, and nearly got gobbled by goats.

9 When Aunt Ruby took us to eat in Restaurant Le Posh – no burgers, no chips, no pizza. Just strange, horrible food in a gloopy sauce. Yuck!

8 When my horrid wormy-worm brother made everyone think I wanted to marry Margaret. I'd rather marry Miss Battle-Axe than marry Margaret.

7 In the haunted house, when I heard spooky sounds coming from the wardrobe.

6 I agreed to eat all my vegetables for FIVE nights in a row, so my horrible parents would take me to Gobble and Go. But when the great day finally arrived, Gobble and Go wasn't there any more!

5 Staying overnight in Our Town Museum, when a creepy monster grabbed my leg in the dark.

4 When I, Horrid Henry, wore frilly pink lacy girls' pants covered in hearts and bows to school – and the latest craze on the playground was de-bagging. Horror of horrors.

3 The night the slimiest, scariest, most horrible and frightening monster in the whole world, the Fangmangler, leaped out of the bushes with a thunderous roar.

2 The day Nurse Needle tried to give me an injection with the longest, sharpest, most wicked needle I'd ever seen.

1 Horrible, horrible Thursday. The class swimming day when I was the only one left alone in the swimming pool – with a shark.

Zombie Chicken Board Game

Zombie Chickens are threatening to ruin Easter by gobbling up all the chocolate eggs. Can you get past them and be the first to reach the big prize egg at the end?

You will need

A counter for each player
Dice
Two or more players

How to Play

1. Each player takes a turn to roll the dice and move from Square 1 around the board.

2. If you land on an Easter egg, move forward by following the red arrow.

3. If you land on a Zombie Chicken, move back by following the red arrow.

4. The winner is the first player to reach the end.

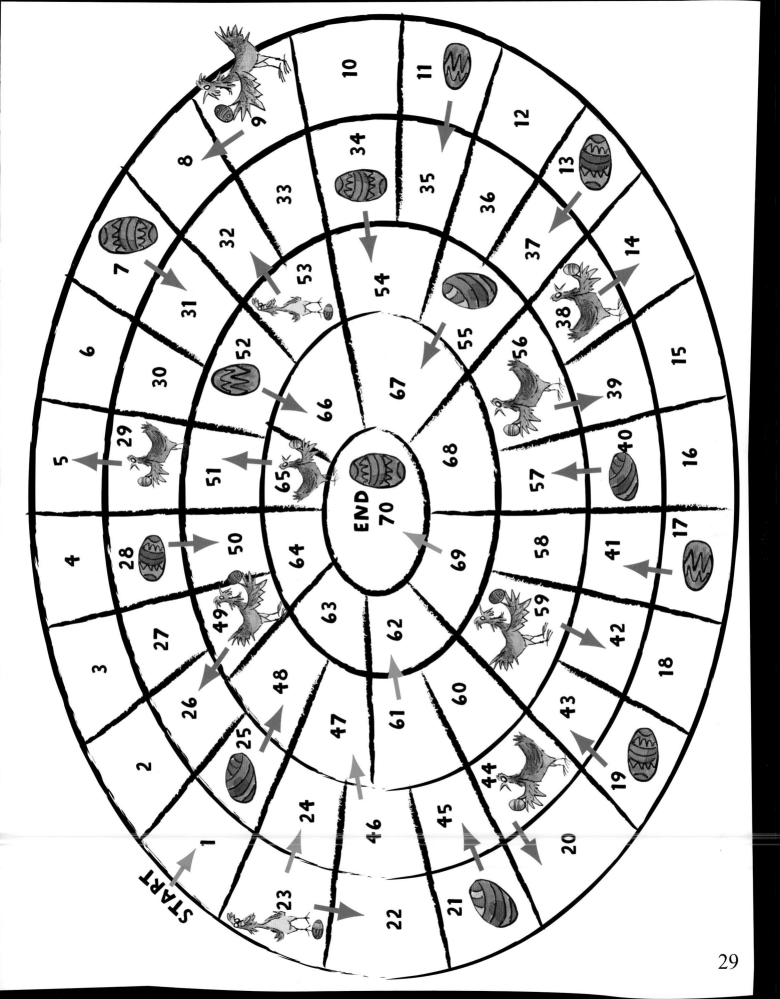

Could You Survive a Zombie Invasion?

1. **Is it better to face zombies as a team or go it alone?**
(a) Stick with your friends. The more of you there are, the better your chance of survival.
(b) Stay together, and obey the leader.
(c) You've got more chance on your own, especially if your team-mates are really rubbish.

2. **How do you decide on a plan of action?**
(a) Talk about it with your team-mates and do something that everyone is happy with.
(b) The leader decides what we're going to do.
(c) Just turn up and see what happens.

3. **A group of zombies have invaded the sweet shop, but you're hungry. What do you do?**
(a) Run away – as far from the sweet shop as you can.
(b) Argue about what to do for so long that the zombies have gobbled up all the sweets and are coming after you!
(c) Hide outside the shop until you think the zombies have gone, then nip in and buy your sweets.

4. **The zombies are coming to your school. What's your plan?**
(a) Escape out of the back door.
(b) Send Miss Battle-Axe to sort them out.
(c) Hide under your desk.

5. **The zombies are shuffling towards your house. Where do you hide?**
(a) In Moody Margaret's tree house – pulling up the ladder behind you.
(b) Behind the sofa.
(c) Under the duvet.

6. **If a zombie catches you, what's the worse thing that could happen?**
(a) It bites you, and you become a zombie too.
(b) It makes you hand over all your pocket money.
(c) It wants to join the Purple Hand Gang and be your best friend.

7. **The zombies are battering down your front door. There's no escape – what do you do?**
(a) Cover yourself in fake blood and pretend to be a zombie.
(b) Scream very loudly and tell them to GO AWAY.
(c) Give in and join them.

8. **You manage to escape the zombie invasion and find a hideaway. What have you brought with you?**
(a) Water, food and blankets.
(b) A pirate hat and cutlass.
(c) A goo-shooter and some day-glo slime.

Count how many (a)s, (b)s and (c)s you've got, then check out your results below to reveal your ideal team and discover your chances of survival.

Mostly (a)s: Welcome to the winning team! The A-TEAM is Aerobic Al, Brainy Brian, Clever Clare and Tough Toby, combining speed, brains and toughness. Perfect for escaping and outwitting the zombies.

Mostly (b)s: Bad luck. You're on the B-TEAM, with Moody Margaret as Team Leader, plus Sour Susan, Gorgeous Gurinder and Singing Soraya. If you do everything Moody Margaret tells you, you'll be able to stay on the team and might even be promoted to Deputy Team Leader. But if you disagree with Margaret, you'll be thrown to the zombies!

Mostly (c)s: Like Horrid Henry, you're too cunning and clever to be on a team with a load of losers. Armed with a trusty goo-shooter and some day-glo slime, you're brave enough to go into battle alone against a million trillion zombies – SPLAT!

Horrid Henry and the Fangmangler

Henry disappeared into the black darkness of the garden.

For a long long moment there was silence.

"This is stupid," said Moody Margaret.

Suddenly, a low, moaning growl echoed through the moonless night.

"What was that?" said Spotless Sam nervously.

"Henry? Are you all right, Henry?" squeaked Perfect Peter.

The low moaning growl turned into a snarl.

THRASH! CRASH!

"HELP! HELP! THE FANGMANGLER'S AFTER ME! RUN FOR YOUR LIVES!" screamed Horrid Henry, smashing through the bushes. His T-shirt and trousers were torn.

The Best Boys Club screamed and ran.

Sour Susan screamed and ran.

Horrid Henry screamed and … stopped.

He waited until he was alone. Then Horrid Henry wiped some ketchup from his face, clutched his bank and did a war dance round the garden, whooping with joy.

"Money! Money! Money! Money! Money!" he squealed, leaping and stomping. He danced and he pranced, he twirled and he whirled. He was so busy dancing and cackling he didn't notice a shadowy shape slip into the garden behind him.

"Money! Money! Money! Mine! Mine – " he broke off. What was that noise? Horrid Henry's throat tightened.

"Hah," he thought. "It's nothing."

Then suddenly a dark shape leapt out of the bushes and let out a thunderous roar.

Horrid Henry shrieked with terror.

Has Horrid Henry really met a Fangmangler? Find out in 'Horrid Henry and the Fangmangler' from Horrid Henry's Nits.

Fangmangler Fun

Answer the clues and fit the words into the crossword puzzle. Each word begins with one of the letters in the word FANGMANGLER.

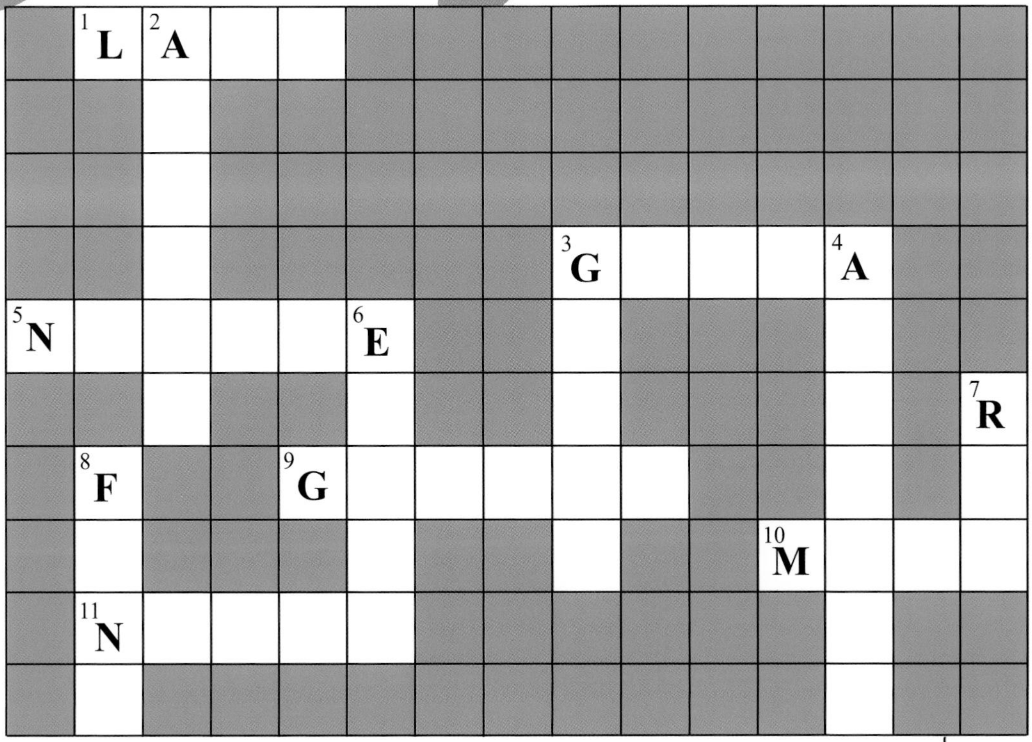

1 L
2 A
3 G
4 A
5 N
6 E
7 R
8 F
9 G
10 M
11 N

Across

1. An old-fashioned light.
3. A girl's name.
5. Something sharp, used for sewing.
9. Covered in oil or butter. Add to 3 across to make a demon dinner lady!
10. Spooks make this sound.
11. Works in a hospital. Add to 5 across to make someone who tries to give Horrid Henry an injection.

Down

2. A boy's name.
3. See-through and haunting.
4. Worried. Add to 2 down to make a nervous character in Henry's class.
6. Spooky and creepy.
7. The best thing do to if you see a Fangmangler!
8. A sharp tooth.

Car Bingo

Horrid Henry loves playing Car Bingo on long car journeys. He and Peter each have to spot all the items out of the window on their side of the car. But it's cheating to look out of the wrong window!

SHEEP	HORRID HAT	DOG	CAT	GLASSES
BABY	DOG	GLASSES	HORRID HAT	BABY
GLASSES	SHEEP	BULL	CAT	GLASSES
HORRID HAT	CAT	DOG	BABY	HORRID HAT
DOG	BABY	CAT	SHEEP	GLASSES

How to play

If one player spots an item, like a sheep, they cross out one of the sheep on their grid. If they see three sheep together, they can cross out all three sheep on the grid. The winner is the first player to cross out a whole line – either across or down.

34

Perfect Peter's Pencil and Paper Game

Peter loves playing quiet pencil and paper games in the back of the car. Here's one of his favourites.

FIRST TO FIVE

How to play

1. Draw a grid on a piece of paper – 10 squares x 10 squares.

2. One player is noughts and the other player is crosses.

3. The youngest player starts. (That's Perfect Peter's rule!).

4. Each player in turn marks a square with their symbol – anywhere on the grid.

5. The first player to get five squares in a row – horizontally, vertically or diagonally – is the winner.

Here's an example. Horrid Henry was the noughts (he broke Peter's rules and went first!). But Perfect Peter was the winner.

Holiday Howlers

Match the words to these holiday jokes. Then fit them into the criss-cross puzzle. One word has already been filled in to help you.

4 letters
COWS
FROG
SAND

6 letters
SUNDAY
NOBODY
MONKEY

5 letters
GREEN
SHEEP

7 letters
MUMMIES
ZOMBIES

WHY DID THE __ __ __ __ SCREAM?
BECAUSE THE SEAWEED.

WHAT'S THE BEST DAY TO GO TO THE BEACH?
— — — — — — .

WHY DON'T **MUMMIES** GO ON HOLIDAY?
THEY ARE AFRAID THEY MIGHT RELAX AND UNWIND.

WHAT'S __ __ __ __ __ AND ROUND AND GOES CAMPING?
A BOY SPROUT.

WHY DIDN'T THE SKELETON GO ON HOLIDAY?
HE HAD __ __ __ __ __ __ TO GO WITH.

WHERE DO __ __ __ __ __ GO ON HOLIDAY?
THE BAA-HAMAS.

WHERE DO __ __ __ __ GO ON HOLIDAY?
MOO-ZEALAND.

WHY DID THE __ __ __ __ __ __ SUNBATHE?
TO GET AN ORANGU-TAN.

HOW DID THE __ __ __ __ CROSS THE CHANNEL?
BY HOPPERCRAFT.

WHERE DO __ __ __ __ __ __ __ GO ON HOLIDAY?
THE DEADITERRANEAN.

CLUE: FILL IN THE LONGEST WORD FIRST.

MUMMIES

Horrid Henry's Camping Survival Guide

Horrid Henry hates family holidays, especially camping.
He'd much rather stay at home, eating crisps and watching TV.
Here are his top survival tips.

BEFORE YOU GO

Pretend to be ill. Then your parents will cancel the holiday, and you can just lie on the sofa and watch TV, while Mum brings you cold drinks and ice cream all day.

If this fails...

- Pack your suitcase very slowly. You might miss the train, plane or ferry, and then you'll be able to stay at home.

- Forget something important like your suitcase. When you arrive at the campsite, your parents will be angry, but you'll still have to come home to get your bag.

- Leave your walking boots behind – by mistake, tee hee!

- Take the things you really need – like your boom-box, your Grisly Ghoul Grub Box and Dungeon Drink Kit, your Super Soaker 2000 water blaster, and lots of comics.

ON THE WAY

Beg your mean, horrible parents to buy a new car, with a *built-in* TV, fast food on tap and a jacuzzi.

If this fails...

• Sneak lots of sweets into the car.

• Hide Perfect Peter's stupid story CDs and bring your own Killer Boy Rats music.

• Tell your parents you NEED to go to the toilet – then pretend to get locked in.

• Ask if you're nearly there yet – about every 10 seconds. Your parents will never want to take you on holiday again.

ON HOLIDAY

• Whine every day – it's too hot, it's too cold, the food is horrible, everything is horrible. Your parents will get so fed up, they'll take you home. Hooray!

• Do a rain dance. When it pours down and washes your tent away, you can leave the cold campsite and move to the brilliant one across the road, with beds, hot baths and heated swimming pools.

• Hide all the disgusting healthy food your parents have *brought* with them so they have to take you to the nearby burger bar.

Greedy Graham's Grisly Grub

FINGER SANDWICHES

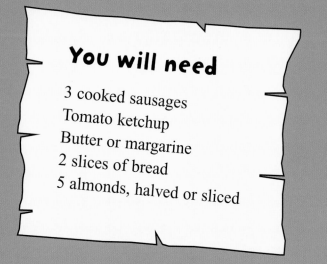

You will need

3 cooked sausages
Tomato ketchup
Butter or margarine
2 slices of bread
5 almonds, halved or sliced

1. Cut the sausages in half lengthways – these are your fingers.

2. Poke an almond half or slice into one end of five of the sausage halves so that they look like fingernails.

3. Butter the bread.

4. Arrange the five fingers on the slice of bread to look like four fingers and a thumb, then squirt on lots of tomato ketchup.

5. Put the other slice of bread on top to make a sandwich, and press it down so that the ketchup (or blood!) oozes out.

BLOODTHIRSTY CELERY

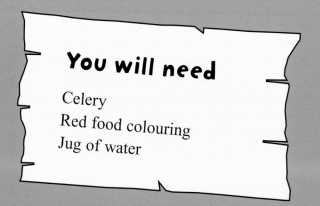

You will need

Celery
Red food colouring
Jug of water

1. Mix a few drops of food colouring with the water.

2. Cut the bottom off the celery and place it in the water.

3. Wait overnight. In the morning the celery will be stripy and look like it's soaked in blood!

EDIBLE EYEBALLS

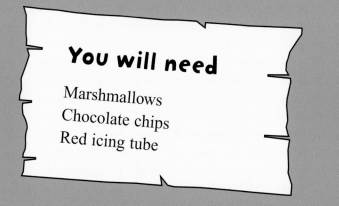

You will need

Marshmallows
Chocolate chips
Red icing tube

1. Push a chocolate chip in the middle of each of the marshmallows.

2. Using the red icing, draw blood vessels around the chocolate chip to make it look like an eye.

Monstrous Menus

Can you work out which of the tasty treats in the list below belongs to which menu?

Brain Burgers
Fried Flesh
Frogface Fritters
Broccoli Buns
Sloppy Mash
Phantom Fries

Snobby Salmon
Snooty Snails
Soggy Semolina
Spinach Surprise
Spooky Spookhetti
Worm Pie

Ghostly Gobble and Go

1. Banshee Burgers
2. Ice Screaming
3. _ _ _ _ _ _ _ _ _ _ _
   _ _ _ _ _ _ _ _
4. _ _ _ _ _ _ _ _ _ _ _ _ _

CLUE:
Look for a tasty treat to eat with burgers, and a scary pasta dish.

Horrid Henry's Nightmare Nosh

1. Sprout Soup
2. Pea and Parsnip Pie
3. _ _ _ _ _ _ _ _ _ _ _
   _ _ _ _ _ _ _ _ _ _ _
4. _ _ _ _ _ _ _ _ _ _ _ _ _

CLUE:
Henry hates vegetables. Find the vile veggie dishes, and you've got his nightmare nosh!

Restaurant Le Posh

1. Best Beetroot Mousse
2. Luxury Lemon Sorbet
3. _ _ _ _ _ _ _ _ _
   _ _ _ _ _ _ _ _ _ _
4. _ _ _ _ _ _ _ _ _ _
   _ _ _ _ _ _ _ _ _

CLUE:
Both of these posh treats are a bit fishy!

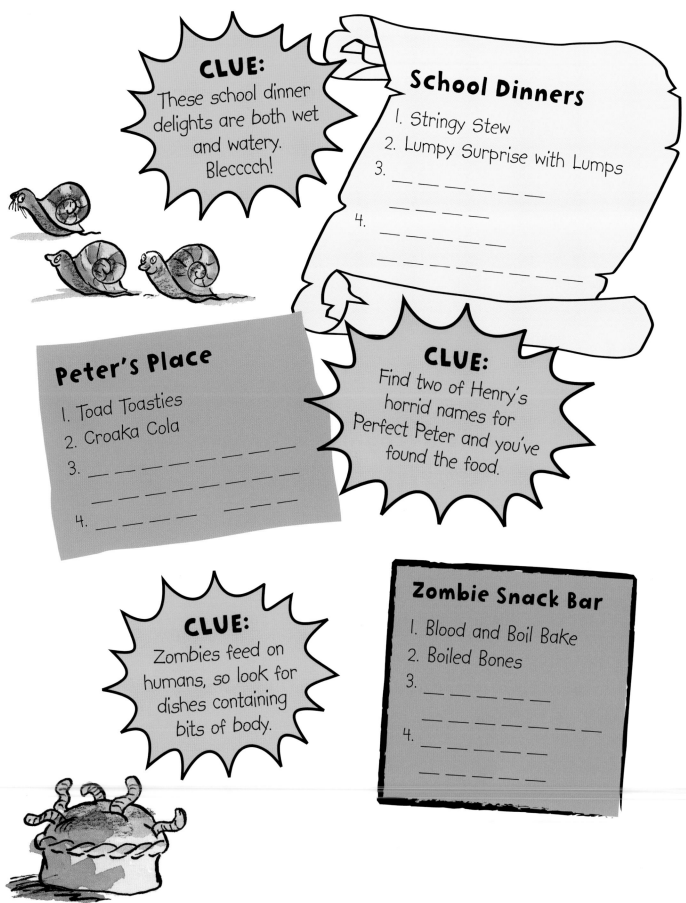

CLUE:
These school dinner delights are both wet and watery. Blecccch!

School Dinners

1. Stringy Stew
2. Lumpy Surprise with Lumps
3. _ _ _ _ _ _ _ _ _ _
   _ _ _ _ _ _ _
4. _ _ _ _ _ _
   _ _ _ _ _ _ _ _

Peter's Place

1. Toad Toasties
2. Croaka Cola
3. _ _ _ _ _ _ _ _ _ _ _
   _ _ _ _ _ _   _ _ _ _
4. _ _ _ _ _ _ _ _

CLUE:
Find two of Henry's horrid names for Perfect Peter and you've found the food.

CLUE:
Zombies feed on humans, so look for dishes containing bits of body.

Zombie Snack Bar

1. Blood and Boil Bake
2. Boiled Bones
3. _ _ _ _ _ _ _
   _ _ _ _ _ _ _ _ _ _
4. _ _ _ _ _ _ _
   _ _ _ _ _ _ _

Scary School

Horrid Henry is back at school, armed with a very special guide for spotting zombie-vampires.

How to Recognise a Vampire

1. Big huge scary teeth
2. Drinks blood
3. Only appears at night
4. Dark clothes
5. Can't see his or her reflection in a mirror
6. Mean and moody
7. Pale skin

How to Recognise a Zombie

1. Looks dead
2. Scary bulging eyes
3. Walks very slowly
4. Doesn't say a lot
5. Feeds on flesh
6. Bad hair

How to recognise a Zombie-Vampire

1. All the above – but being half-zombie means they can walk about in daylight. Help!

Likely Suspects

1. MISS BATTLE-AXE
Dark clothes, big pointy teeth.

2. LAZY LINDA
Sleeps a lot, possibly in a coffin?

3. MOODY MARGARET
Definitely mean and moody.

4. BEEFY BERT
Walks very slowly and only says, "I dunno".

5. NEW NICK
Parents wear strange clothes, and his house is very dark, cold and messy.

6. ANXIOUS ANDREW
Very pale skin, never smiles – he could be hiding his fangs.

Unlikely Suspects

1. MISS LOVELY
She's a vegetarian.

2. GORGEOUS GURINDER
Spends a lot of time looking at her reflection in mirrors.

3. GREASY GRETA
Eats too many crisps and biscuits, and not enough flesh.

4. AEROBIC AL
Too sporty and loves fresh air.

5. JOLLY JOSH
Too cheerful.

Demon Doodles

Turn Henry's enemies into zombie vampires!

Doodle Tips

• Make their skin look grey and dead

• Give them coarse, matted hair

• Add long, pointed fangs

• Add long, sharp fingernails

• Make their eyes look big and bulging

• Give them a black cloak

• Add blood!

A Gallery of Ghouls

Draw your own zombie-vampire

Spooky Sleepover Maze

Henry has lost the rest of his class during a sleepover in the
Town Museum. Can you help him find them?

START

Miss Battle-Axe's Bony Wordsearch

Miss Battle-Axe has set a tricky test full of mind-boggling bone names. Can you find them in the wordsearch puzzle?

SKULL
FEMUR
PELVIC
SPINE
THIGH
PATELLA

TIBIA
RIBS
HUMERUS
STERNUM
CLAVICLE
SCAPULA

A	W	H	S	A	B	E	T	H	P
E	L	J	U	C	K	N	G	S	E
K	R	L	R	M	A	I	W	G	L
D	H	U	E	I	H	P	R	N	V
O	P	J	M	T	B	S	U	P	I
A	O	U	U	E	A	S	X	L	C
Q	C	Y	H	E	F	P	Y	C	A
E	L	C	I	V	A	L	C	L	I
S	T	E	R	N	U	M	U	H	E
L	L	U	K	S	T	I	B	I	A

Autumn School Fair

Here are some of Henry's top money-making schemes for his school fair – they're great games, but even better because people will have to pay to play!

How Many Sweets?

Put sweets in a jar and ask people to guess how many sweets are inside it. At the end of the fair, the closest guess is the winner. When you check the number, it's a good chance to scoff lots of sweets!

Guess the Name of Perfect Peter's Bunny

The first person to guess the correct name is the winner. But if you don't tell the winner they've won, you can carry on taking cash from people all day!

Treasure Hunt

Draw a treasure map and mark numbered squares on it. Decide which square of the map has the treasure, then write the number on a piece of paper and put it in an envelope. At the fair, make a list of which square each person chooses (once they've handed over their money of course). The person who chooses the treasure square wins a prize.

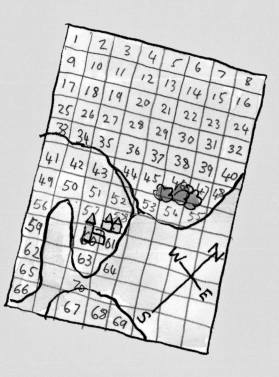

Car Park Carwash

All you need is a bucket of water and a sponge. Charge the parents loads of cold hard cash for giving their cars a quick clean.

Cake Stall

Encourage everyone to make cakes or biscuits, and sell them. Top favourites are Sour Susan's Bitter Lemon Biscuits, Miss Lovely's Butterfly Buns and Greedy Graham's Double Chocolate Monster Muffins.

Beat the Goalie

Set up a goal and offer three balls to beat the goalie. Put Moody Margaret in goal, and you won't have to give away any prizes at all! Ha ha!

Which Hallowe'en Horror Are You?

1. What kind of clothes would you wear on Hallowe'en?

(a) Anything torn and dirty.
(b) A white sheet.
(c) A long black velvet cloak.
(d) A long black dress and a tall black hat.
(e) Something pink and fluffy.

2. What's your favourite treat?

(a) Chocolate fingers.
(b) Marshmallows.
(c) Neck-tarines.
(d) Sand-witches.
(e) Tangerines.

4. What do you like best about Hallowe'en?

(a) Scaring people in the streets.
(b) Haunting your friends and family.
(c) Escaping from your coffin for the night.
(d) Flying around on your broomstick.
(e) Having fun with friends.

3. What's your best trick?

(a) Stuffing a glove with cotton wool, shaking hands with your victim and leaving your hand behind.
(b) Tapping on the window and shouting 'whoooooo'.
(c) Dripping fake blood from your mouth.
(d) Waving your wand and turning your friend into a frog.
(e) Saying 'boo!' quietly, and running away.

5. What *don't* you like about Hallowe'en?
(a) People who hide in their houses.
(b) It's hard to be scary because no one's surprised to see you.
(c) The streets are too busy, and you like to be alone.
(d) Nothing – it's the best night of the year!
(e) It's dark and scary, and everyone eats too many sweets.

6. What's your favourite food?
(a) Brains
(b) Spookhetti
(c) Blood
(d) Stew cooked in a cauldron
(e) Vegetables

Count up how many (a)s, (b)s, (c)s, (d)s and (e)s you got.

Mostly (a)s
You're a brilliant brain-munching zombie!

Mostly (b)s
You're a spooky spine-tingling ghost – whooooo-ooooooooo!

Mostly (c)s
You're a fangtastically vicious vampire.

Mostly (d)s
You're a spellbinding wicked witch.

Mostly (e)s
You're a perfectly pink fluffy bunny!

53

A Big Bad Bat Mobile

You will need

1 sheet of black paper or cardboard

Black thread, cut into six lengths

Craft glue

Coat hanger

String

Scissors

Greaseproof or tracing paper

Pencil

Googly eyes (optional)

CRAFTY TIP:
CUT THE BATS OUT FROM BLACK FELT INSTEAD AND PIN THEM TO YOUR CURTAINS.

Instructions

1. Trace the bat template onto the paper. Cut out the template, and draw round it six times on the black cardboard. Cut out the six bats.

2. Fold the bats in half in the centre along the dotted line on the template. Also fold both wings along the dotted lines.

3. If you have them, you can stick googly eyes on your bats.

4. Place a blob of glue in the middle of each of the bats, then press a piece of black thread onto each of the blobs.

3. Let the glue dry completely, then tie your bats to the coat hanger, so that they are spread out evenly and hang at different lengths.

5. Hang up your mobile – perfect for scaring people who dare to enter your bedroom!

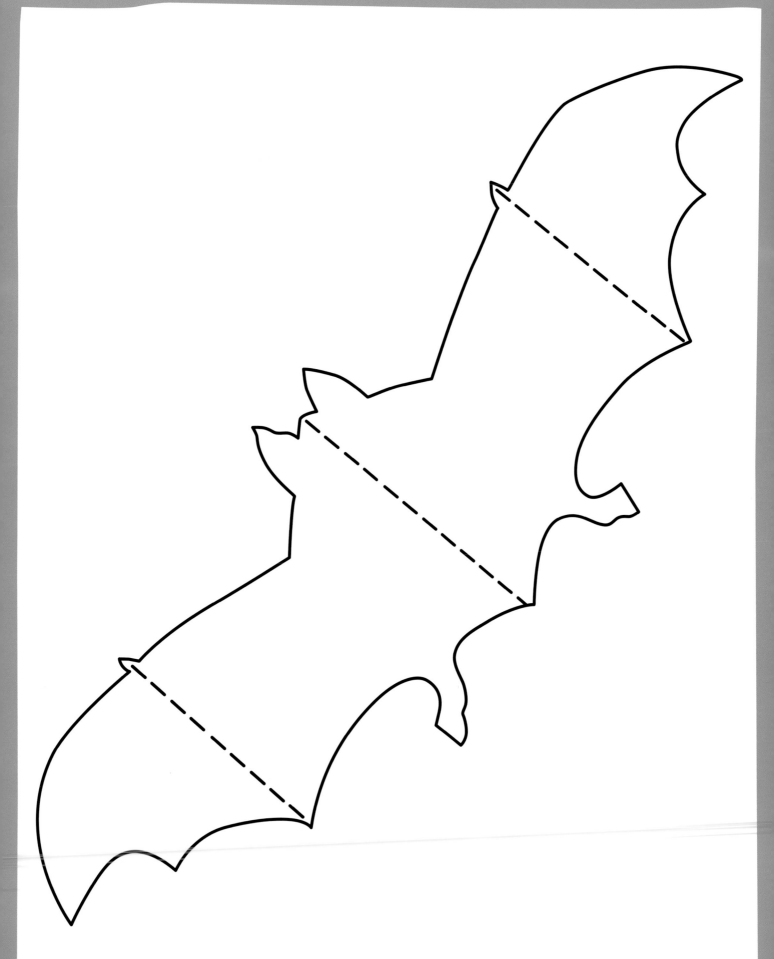

55

Horrid Henry's Haunted House

Henry lay in bed. Somehow he'd survived the dreadful meal and Stuck-up Steve's bragging about his expensive clothes, toys and trainers. Now here he was, alone in the attic at the top of the house. He'd jumped into bed, carefully avoiding the faded brown patch on the floor. He was sure it was just spilled cola or something, but just in case …

Henry looked around him. The only thing he didn't like was the huge wardrobe opposite the bed. It loomed up in the darkness at him. You could hide a body in that wardrobe, thought Henry, then rather wished he hadn't.

"Ooooooooh."

Henry stiffened.

Had he just imagined the sound of someone moaning?

Silence.

Nothing, thought Henry, snuggling down under the covers. Just the wind.

"Ooooooooooh."

This time the moaning was a fraction louder. The hairs on Henry's neck stood up. He gripped the sheets tightly.

"Haaaaaahhhhhhh."

Henry sat up.

"Haaaaaaaaahhhhhhhhhhhh."

The ghostly breathy moaning sound was not coming from outside. It appeared to be coming from inside the giant wardrobe.

Quickly, Henry switched on the bedside light.

What am I going to do? thought Henry. He wanted to run screaming to his aunt.

But the truth was, Henry was too frightened to move.

Some dreadful moaning thing was inside the wardrobe.

Just waiting to get *him*.

What is the dreadful moaning thing hiding in the wardrobe? Find out in **'Horrid Henry's Haunted House'** from *Horrid Henry's Haunted House*.

Zombie Sudoku

Every row, column and mini-grid must contain the letters Z O M B I E.

B					I
		O	Z		
	Z	M		B	
	I			E	
		E	B		
M			O		E

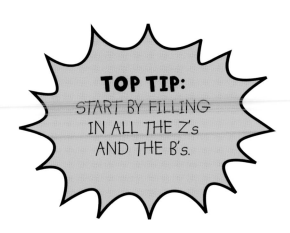

TOP TIP:
START BY FILLING
IN ALL THE Z's
AND THE B's.

57

Monstrous Makeovers

Zombie

- Wear ripped and tattered old clothes.
- Rub dirt on the clothes and splatter them with red paint or fake blood.
- For your face, mix up a scary grey colour by adding a tiny bit of black face paint to white. Paint this all over your face.
- Paint black rings around your eyes.
- Mess up your hair with gel.

Now you look as though you've just arisen from a grave – dirty, dishevelled and dead. Practise walking very slowly with your arms stretched out in front of you. No laughing or smiling allowed!

Vampire

- Black clothes are best for vampires – trousers and a waistcoat for boys, a long dress for a girl.
- Wear a long black cloak and carry a cane.
- Use white face paint or powder on your face, with dark red or black lips.
- Don't forget some fangs and a dribble of fake blood.

Slink around in the shadows, looking mean and mysterious. Avoid garlic and mirrors.

Mummy

- Use bandages or an old white sheet cut up into long strips. If you're really stuck, you can use toilet roll.
- Put on plain white clothes, like a t-shirt and trousers.
- Wrap the bandages, sheet strips or toilet roll around you. Pin carefully to your clothes with safety pins when you need to start a new piece.
- Paint your face with white face paint, and just wrap a few bandages around your head, so you can see where you're going.

Practise walking as though you've been trapped in a tomb for thousands of years.

Gorgeous Gurinder

Sour Susan

Ghost

- Take an old white sheet and cut a hole in the middle to put your head through.
- Paint your face with white face paint, with black around your eyes.
- Put white talcum powder in your hair to give a ghostly effect.
- You could wear old-fashioned white clothes instead of a sheet – like a suit for a boy or an old bridesmaid's dress for a girl.

Before you head off trick or treating, try haunting your family at home first! Whooooo!

Tangled Trick or Treating

Follow the tangled strings to find out who gets
the crisps, the sweets or the tangerines.

Hallowe'en Loot

Horrid Henry has hidden his Hallowe'en sweets in his bedroom so that no one else can get their hands on them. And he's hidden tangerines so that Mum can't make him eat them! How many can you find?

Horrid Henry's Family and Friends' Greatest Fears

Peter

Leaving home without a hanky
Getting his clothes dirty
A day without homework
Being told off

Mum

Spiders
Having her boss to dinner
Meeting Henry's teacher

Dad

Needles
Tomatoes
Meeting Henry's teacher

Stuck-up Steve
Wearing second-hand clothes
Monsters under the bed

Rude Ralph
Meeting someone ruder than him

Moody Margaret
Being outwitted by Henry

Horrid Henry
Injections
Being outwitted by Margaret

Sour Susan
That Margaret won't be her best friend any more

Horrid Henry's Christmas Presents

"I've bought and wrapped all my presents, Mum," said Perfect Peter.
"I've been saving my pocket money for months."

"Whoopee for you," said Henry.

"Henry, it's always better to give than to receive," said Peter.

Mum beamed. "Quite right, Peter."

"Says who?" growled Horrid Henry. "I'd much rather *get* presents."

"Don't be so horrid, Henry," said Mum.

"Don't be so selfish, Henry," said Dad.

Horrid Henry stuck out his tongue. Mum and Dad gasped.

"You horrid boy," said Mum.

"I just hope Father Christmas didn't see that," said Dad.

"Henry," said Peter, "Father Christmas won't bring you any presents if you're bad."

"Aaaarrrgghhh!" Horrid Henry sprang at Peter. He was a grizzly bear guzzling a juicy morsel.

"AAAAHEEE," wailed Peter. "Henry pinched me."

"Henry! Go to your room," said Mum.

"Fine!" screamed Horrid Henry, stomping off and slamming the door. Why did he get stuck with the world's meanest and most horrible parents? *They* certainly didn't deserve any presents.

Presents! Why couldn't he just *get* them? Why oh why did he have to *give* them? Giving other people presents was such a waste of his hard-earned money. Every time he gave a present it meant something he couldn't buy for himself. Goodbye chocolate. Goodbye comics. Goodbye Deluxe Goo-Shooter. And then, if you bought anything good, it was so horrible having to give it away. He'd practically cried having to give Ralph that Terminator Gladiator poster for his birthday. And the Mutant Max lunchbox Mum made him give Kasim still made him gnash his teeth whenever he saw Kasim with it.

Now he was stuck, on Christmas Eve, with no money, and no presents to give anyone, deserving or not.

How does Henry solve his Christmas present problem? Find out in **'Horrid Henry's Christmas Presents'** from **Horrid Henry's Christmas Cracker**.

A Star is Born

Do you have star quality or are you best in the back row?

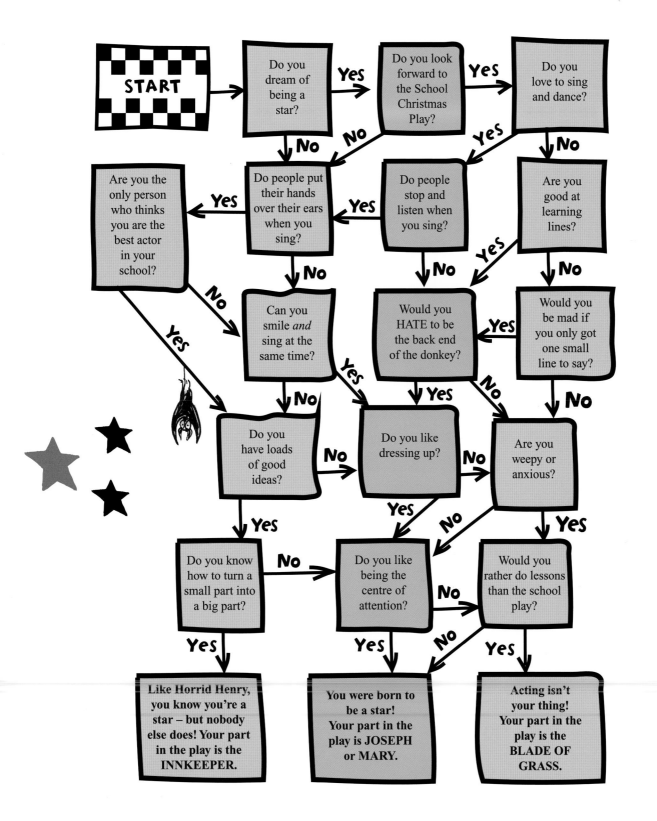

START

Do you dream of being a star?
— Yes → Do you look forward to the School Christmas Play?
— No → Do people put their hands over their ears when you sing?

Do you look forward to the School Christmas Play?
— Yes → Do you love to sing and dance?
— No → Do people put their hands over their ears when you sing?

Do you love to sing and dance?
— Yes → Do people stop and listen when you sing?
— No → Are you good at learning lines?

Are you the only person who thinks you are the best actor in your school?
— Yes → Do people put their hands over their ears when you sing?
— Yes → Do you have loads of good ideas?

Do people put their hands over their ears when you sing?
— Yes → Are you the only person who thinks you are the best actor in your school?
— No → Can you smile *and* sing at the same time?

Do people stop and listen when you sing?
— Yes → Do people put their hands over their ears when you sing?
— No → Would you HATE to be the back end of the donkey?

Are you good at learning lines?
— Yes → Would you HATE to be the back end of the donkey?
— No → Would you be mad if you only got one small line to say?

Can you smile *and* sing at the same time?
— Yes → Do you like dressing up?
— No → Do you have loads of good ideas?

Would you HATE to be the back end of the donkey?
— Yes → Do you like dressing up?
— No → Are you weepy or anxious?

Would you be mad if you only got one small line to say?
— Yes → Would you HATE to be the back end of the donkey?
— No → Are you weepy or anxious?

Do you have loads of good ideas?
— No → Do you like dressing up?
— Yes → Do you know how to turn a small part into a big part?

Do you like dressing up?
— Yes → Do you like being the centre of attention?
— No → Are you weepy or anxious?

Are you weepy or anxious?
— No → Do you like being the centre of attention?
— Yes → Would you rather do lessons than the school play?

Do you know how to turn a small part into a big part?
— No → Do you like being the centre of attention?
— Yes → **Like Horrid Henry, you know you're a star – but nobody else does! Your part in the play is the INNKEEPER.**

Do you like being the centre of attention?
— No → Would you rather do lessons than the school play?
— Yes → **You were born to be a star! Your part in the play is JOSEPH or MARY.**

Would you rather do lessons than the school play?
— No → **You were born to be a star! Your part in the play is JOSEPH or MARY.**
— Yes → **Acting isn't your thing! Your part in the play is the BLADE OF GRASS.**

Like Horrid Henry, you know you're a star – but nobody else does! Your part in the play is the INNKEEPER.

You were born to be a star! Your part in the play is JOSEPH or MARY.

Acting isn't your thing! Your part in the play is the BLADE OF GRASS.

Creepy Christmas List Wordsearch

Horrid Henry wants to look like a zombie vampire at Christmas. He's made a list of everything he needs. Find them in the wordsearch. The first 11 leftover letters reveal what he really has to dress up in!

FANGS
CLOAK
MASK
BLOOD
WIG

MIRROR
WAISTCOAT
MEDALLION
TAILCOAT
MAKEUP

T	A	I	L	C	O	A	T	P
K	A	O	L	C	A	P	F	U
M	R	O	R	R	I	M	A	E
I	A	G	C	B	N	K	N	K
B	I	S	O	T	L	W	G	A
W	T	I	K	E	S	O	S	M
M	E	D	A	L	L	I	O	N
H	L	U	E	X	M	D	A	D
A	D	W	Z	S	M	Y	V	W

Fill in the first 11 leftover letters below.

— — — — — — — — — — —

66

Sticky Spider Webs

Forget soppy snowflakes – Horrid Henry is making a glittery spider's web, complete with a creepy-crawly spider.

You will need

Greaseproof paper
Pen or pencil
Gold glitter glue

Instructions

1. Draw a spider's web and a spider (separately) on the greaseproof paper.

2. Paint over your design with the gold glitter glue. Use thick lines so that the web and the spider's legs won't break, then leave them to dry overnight.

3. When they feel dry, peel your web and spider away from the paper. (If some of the glue is still wet underneath, turn them over and leave to dry again.)

4. When it's all completely dry, glue your spider to the web and leave it to dry again.

5. Hang your web in the window with ribbon or string, or tape it to the window.

Clever Clare's Christmas Quiz

1. **What are the two most popular Christmas colours?**
(a) Black and white
(b) Orange and purple
(c) Red and green

2. **How many days are there on a traditional Advent Calendar?**
(a) 24
(b) 25
(c) 12

3. **What is sometimes hidden in a Christmas pudding?**
(a) A smelly sock
(b) A coin
(c) A Gold Gotcha

4. **What should Horrid Henry do under the mistletoe?**
(a) Pounce on Perfect Peter
(b) Kiss Rich Aunt Ruby
(c) Sing Killer Boy Rats songs

6. **What were Victorian Christmas trees decorated with?**
(a) Mega-flashing fairy lights
(b) Candles
(c) Sprouts

5. **What should you leave out for the reindeer?**
(a) Sprouts
(b) Cabbage
(c) Carrots

7. What's an old name for Christmas pudding?

(a) Plum pudding

(b) Rancid raisin pudding

(c) Gloppy globule pudding

9. Why do we shorten the word 'Christmas' to 'Xmas'?

(a) Christmas takes too long to write

(b) It's easier to spell

(c) X is the first letter of the Greek word for Christ

8. How did Boxing Day get its name?

(a) A boxing match was always held on that day

(b) Money that had been collected in boxes was given to poor people on that day

(c) Children who had behaved badly on Christmas Day were thrown into boxes to give the grown-ups some peace and quiet

10. 'A Christmas Carol' by Charles Dickens has some very creepy characters in it. What are they?

(a) Ghosts

(b) Goblins

(c) Zombie-Vampires

How did you do? Find out on page 75.

7 – 10

Congratulations! You're as clued-up about Christmas as Clever Clare.

4 – 6

Not bad – you nearly know your turkey from your tinsel.

1 – 3

Uh-oh! You're just Christmas crackers!

A Night in the Museum

Horrid Henry's class is spending the night in Our Town Museum. It's dull during the day, but when darkness falls it becomes spooky and scary!

Scary Successes

Horrid Henry has been horrid and scary all year. But which were his super successes and which ones ended in disaster? Why not add in your own list too?

HENRY'S LIST	YOUR LIST
Sneaking up on the Secret Club and scaring Margaret and Susan. Purple Hand rules!	
Hiding worms in Peter's bed every night.	
Telling Peter a ghost story before he went to bed – nappy pants wibble worm.	
De-bagging Tough Toby in the school playground. Tee hee.	
Scaring Rabid Rebecca with a creepy-crawly spider.	
Tricking Stuck-up Steve into believing his house is haunted.	
Jumping out at Mum and hearing her scream.	
Driving Dad mad with the Killer Boy Rats on at top volume. Brilliant fun – until he banished my boom-box.	
Frightening Peter and his goody-goody Best Boys by telling them about the Fangmangler – until it really did leap out of the bushes and attack me.	

SUPER SUCCESSES

DISASTERS

BOOM BOOM

Answers

Page 11

There are 8 vampire bats hidden in the Annual.

Page 14

1. (b)
2. (c)
3. (a)
4. (c)
5. (a)
6. (b)
7. (b)
8. (c)

Page 21

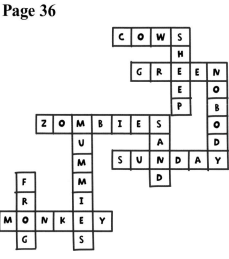

Page 33

Page 20

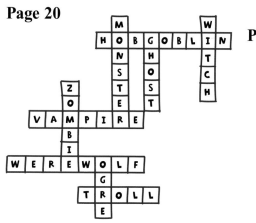

Page 36

Page 42

Ghostly Gobble and Go
Phantom Fries
Spooky Spookhetti

Nightmare Nosh
Spinach Surprise
Broccoli Buns

Restaurant Le Posh
Snobby Salmon
Snooty Snails

School Dinners
Sloppy Mash
Soggy Semolina

Peter's Place
Frogface Fritters
Worm Pie

Zombie Snack Bar
Brain Burgers
Fried Flesh

Page 48

START

Page 49

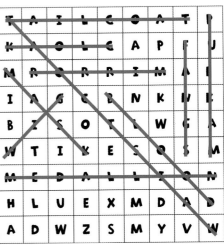

Page 57

B	M	Z	E	O	I
I	E	O	Z	M	B
E	Z	M	I	B	O
O	I	B	M	E	Z
Z	O	E	B	I	M
M	B	I	O	Z	E

Page 60

Horrid Henry = tangerines
Weepy William = crisps
Perfect Peter = sweets

Page 61

5 sweets
5 tangerines

Page 66

A PINK BOW TIE.

Page 68

1. (c)
2. (a)
3. (b)
4. (b)
5. (c)
6. (b)
7. (a)
8. (b)
9. (c)
10. (a)

You can read these other *Horrid Henry* titles, stories available as audio editions, read by Miranda Richardson